BOO

WA

JOKES

This is a Parragon Book
First published in 2003

Parragon
Queen Street House
4 Queen Street
Bath BA1 1HE
UK

Copyright © Parragon 2003

Produced by Magpie Books, an imprint of
Constable & Robinson Ltd, London

Illustrations © David Mostyn

ISBN 1- 40540-621-6

A copy of the British Library Cataloguing-in-Publication Data
is available from the British Library

Printed in China

Contents

Mean and Nasty Jokes

The garbage men were just about to leave the street when a woman came running out of the house carrying some cardboard boxes. "Am I too late for the garbage?" she called.

"No, lady," replied one of the men. "Jump right in!"

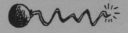

Girl: Did you like that cake Mrs Jones?

Mrs Jones: Yes, very much.

Girl: That's funny. My mom said you didn't have any taste.

A woman woke her husband in the middle of the night. "There's a burglar downstairs eating the cake that I made this morning."

"Who shall I call," her husband said, "police or ambulance?"

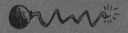

Fred: I was sorry to hear that your mother-in-law had died. What was the complaint?

Ted: We haven't had any yet.

When you leave school, you should become a bone specialist. You've certainly got the head for it.

My auntie Maud had so many candles on her last birthday cake that all her party guests got sunburnt.

When Wally Witherspoon proposed
to his girlfriend she said:
"I love the simple things in life,
Wally, but I don't want one of them
for a husband."

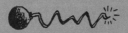

Two friends were discussing the
latest scandalous revelations
about a Hollywood actress.
"They say she likes her latest
husband so much she's decided to
keep him for another month," said
one to the other.

Roger was in a very full bus when a fat woman opposite said, "If you were a gentleman, young man, you'd stand up and let someone else sit down."

"And if you were a lady," replied Roger, "you'd stand up and let four people sit down."

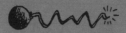

My son's just received a scholarship to medical school – but they don't want him while he's alive.

My mother uses lemon juice for her complexion. Maybe that's why she always looks so sour.

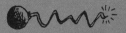

My auntie Mabel has got so many double chins it looks like she is peering over a pile of crumpets.

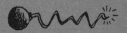

Chuck: Do you have holes in your underpants?
Teacher: No, of course not.
Chuck: Then how do you get your feet through?

My girlfriend talks so much that when she goes on holiday, she has to spread suntan lotion on her tongue.

At my piano teacher's last performance the audience cheered and cheered. The piano was locked!

A school inspector was talking to a pupil. "How many teachers work in this school?" he asked.
"Only about half of them, I reckon," replied the pupil.

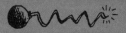

Father: Would you like me to help you with your homework?
Son: No thanks, I'd rather get it wrong by myself.

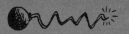

I wouldn't say our English teacher is fat, but when she got on a Speak Your Weight machine it surrendered.

Rob: I must rush home and cut the lawn.
Teacher: Did your father promise you something if you cut it?
Rob: No, he promised me something if I didn't!

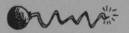

She's such a gossip she tells you what you were going to say to her before you have the chance to tell her.

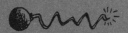

I have two noses, three eyes and only one ear. What am I?
Very ugly.

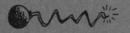

Mrs Broadbeam: Now, remember, children, travel is very good for you. It broadens the mind.
Sarah, muttering: If you're anything to go by, that's not all it broadens!

Why is a caretaker nothing like Robinson Crusoe?
Because Robinson Crusoe got all his work done by Friday.

"Did you see him?" asked the policeman.

"No," said Mrs Blenkinsop, "but I'd know that laugh anywhere."

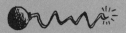

I can't get over that new beard of yours. It makes your face look just like a busted sofa.

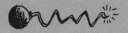

Henry: I'd like to learn to play a drum, Sir.

Music Teacher: Beat it!

What do you get if you pour boiling
water down a rabbit hole?
Hot cross bunnies.

Yes, I do like your dress – but isn't it a little early for Hallowe'en?

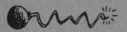

You must think I'm a perfect idiot. No, you're not perfect.

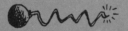

Soprano at concert: And what would you like me to sing next?
Member of audience: Do you know "Old Man River"?
Soprano: Er, yes.
Member of audience: Well go jump in it.

I don't care who you are, get those reindeer off my roof.

I don't know what it is that makes you stupid but whatever it is, it works.

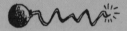

My dad is rather tired this morning. Last night he dreamed he was working.

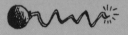

Wife: Shall I give that tramp one of my cakes?
Husband: Why, what harm has he ever done us?

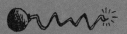

My uncle spent a fortune on deodorants before he found out that people didn't like him anyway.

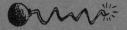

What is small, pink, wrinkly, and belongs to Grandpa?
Grandma.

Why don't you go home and brush up on your ignorance?

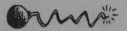

How does your head feel today?
As good as new.
It should be as good as new – it's never been used.

My uncle must be the meanest man in the world. He recently found a crutch – then he broke his leg so he could use it.

I've got a good idea.
Must be beginner's luck.

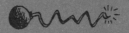

I reckon mom must be at least 30
years old – I counted the rings
under her eyes.

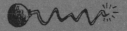

Woman: If you were my husband
I'd poison your coffee.
Man: And if you were my wife, I'd
drink it.

Visitor: You're very quiet, Jennifer.
Jennifer: Well, my mom gave me 10 cents not to say anything about your red nose.

Mom! There's a man at the door collecting for the Old Folks' Home. Shall I give him Grandma?

I've just finished painting your portrait. There, don't you think it looks like you?
Er . . . well . . . it probably looks better from a distance.
I told you it was like you!

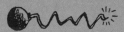

The new office-boy came into his boss's office and said, "I think you're wanted on the phone, sir."
"What d'you mean, you think?" demanded the boss.
"Well, sir, the phone rang, I answered it and a voice said, 'Is that you, you old fool?'"

Billy: I never had a sledge when I was a kid. We were too poor.
Milly, feeling sorry for him: What a shame! What did you do when it snowed?
Billy: Slid down the hills on my cousin.

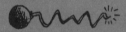

Do you think, Professor, that my wife should take up the piano as a career?
No, I think she should put down the lid as a favor.

Why did you refuse to marry
Richard, Tessa?
'Cos he said he would die if I
didn't and I'm just curious.

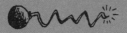

My Peter keeps telling everyone
he's going to marry the most
beautiful girl in the world.
What a shame! And after all the
time you've been engaged!

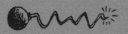

Doctor Sawbones speaking.
Oh, doctor, my wife's just
dislocated her jaw. Can you come
over in, say, three or four weeks'
time?

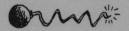

"How should I have played that
last shot?" the bad golfer asked
his partner.
"Under an assumed name."

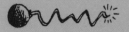

May I go swimming, Mommy?
No, you may not. There are sharks
here.
But Daddy's swimming.
He's insured.

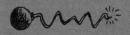

Alfie had been listening to his
sister practice her singing. "Sis,"
he said, "I wish you'd sing
Christmas carols."
"That's nice of you Alfie," she said,
"why?"
"Then I'd only have to hear you
once a year!"

A rather stern aunt had been staying with Sharon's parents, and one day she said to the little girl, "Well, Sharon, I'm going tomorrow. Are you sorry?"

"Oh yes, Auntie," replied Sharon. "I thought you were going today."

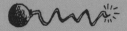

A scoutmaster asked one of his troop what good deed he had done for the day. "Well Skip," said the scout, "Mom had only one dose of castor oil left, so I let my baby brother have it."

The apprentice electrician was on his first job. "Take hold of those two wires, Alex," said his master, "and rub them together."

Alex did as he was bid, and his master said, "Do you feel anything?"

"No," said Alex.

"That's good – so don't touch those other two wires or you'll get a nasty shock!"

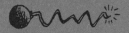

A naughty child was irritating all the passengers on the flight from London to New York. Finally, one man could stand it no longer. "Hey kid," he shouted, "why don't you go outside and play?"

Mr Brown: I hate to tell you, but your wife just fell in the wishing well.
Mr Smith: It works!

Did you hear about the woman who was so ugly she could make yogurt by staring at a pint of milk for an hour?

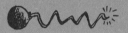

"Some girls think I'm handsome," said the young Romeo, "and some girls think I'm ugly. What do you think, Sheila?"
"A bit of both. Pretty ugly."

You're ugly!
And you're drunk!
Yes, but in the morning I'll be
sober!

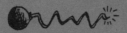

I don't think these photographs
you've taken do me justice.
You don't want justice – you want
mercy!

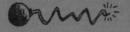

Word Play

Flash Harry gave his girlfriend a mink stole for her birthday. Well, it may not have been mink, but it's fairly certain it was stole.

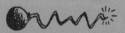

Did you hear about the florist who had two children?
One's a budding genius and the other's a blooming idiot.

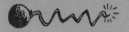

Why is a classroom like an old car?
Because it's full of nuts, and has a
crank at the front.

Where can you dance in
California?
San Fran-disco.

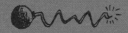

What did the children do when
there were rock cakes for lunch?
Took their pick.

1st Undertaker: I've just been given the sack.
2nd Undertaker: Why?
1st Undertaker: I buried someone in the wrong place.
2nd Undertaker: That was a grave mistake.

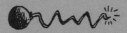

What should you give short elves?
Elf-raising flour.

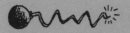

How do we know that Rome was built at night?
Because all the books say it wasn't built in a day!

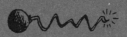

Ben's dad was building a pine bookcase, and Ben was watching and occasionally helping. "What are the holes for?" Ben asked. "They're knot holes," said his dad. "What are they, then, if they're not holes?" said Ben.

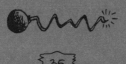

Why do barbers make good drivers?
Because they know all the short cuts.

What's the difference between a square peg in a round hole and a kilo of lard?
One's a fat lot of good and the other's a good lot of fat!

What happens when business is
slow at a medicine factory?
You can hear a cough drop.

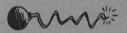

What do you get if you cross a
witch with an ice cube?
A cold spell.

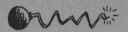

Which two letters are rotten for
your teeth?
D K.

What did the "just married" spiders call their new home? Newlywebs.

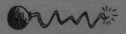

Sign on the school noticeboard: Guitar for sale, cheap, no strings attached.

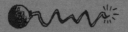

Darren, at school dinner: I've just swallowed a bone.
Teacher: Are you choking?
Darren: No, I'm serious.

Girl: Shall I put the kettle on?
Boy: No, I think you look alright in the dress you're wearing.

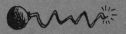

What do you get if you cross a caretaker with a monk who smokes large cigars?
A caretaker with a bad habit.

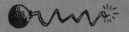

Who carries a sack and bites people?
Santa Jaws.

Sign outside the school caretaker's hut: Will the person who took my ladder please return it, or further steps will be taken.

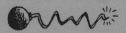

When George left school he was going to be a printer. All the teachers said he was the right type.

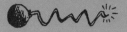

What's the difference between an iced lolly and the school bully? You lick one, the other licks you.

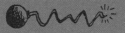

Teacher to Dinner Lady: A pork chop, please and make it lean. Dinner Lady: Certainly, Mr Smith, which way?

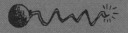

Why did the man go out and buy a set of tools?
Because everyone kept telling him he had a screw loose.

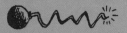

What's the difference between a nail and a boxer?
One gets knocked in, the other gets knocked out.

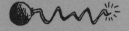

A pilot flying over the jungle was having trouble with his plane and decided to bail out before it crashed. So he got into his parachute, jumped, pulled the rip-cord, and drifted gently down to land. Unfortunately he landed right in a large cooking pot which a tribal chief was simmering gently over a fire. The chief looked at him, rubbed his eyes, looked again, and asked, "What's this flier doing in my soup?"

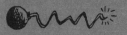

Two fleas were sitting on Robinson
Crusoe's back as he lay on the
beach in the sun. "Well, so long,"
said one to the other, "I'll see you
on Friday."

Two fishermen were out in their
boat one day when a hand
appeared in the ocean.
"What's that?" asked the first
fisherman. "It looks as if
someone's drowning!"
"Nonsense," said the second. "It
was just a little wave."

What kind of bandage do people
wear after heart surgery?
Ticker tape.

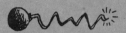

What chocolate treat would you
find at the bottom of the sea?
Oyster eggs.

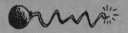

What goes "Ooooooo"?
A cow with no lips.

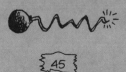

What happened to Ray when a ten-ton truck ran over him?
He became X-Ray.

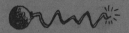

Did you hear about the boy who got worried when his nose grew to eleven inches long?
He thought it might turn into a foot.

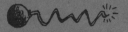

What do you do if you split your
sides laughing?
Run until you get a stitch.

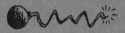

Do undertakers enjoy their job?
Of corpse they do.

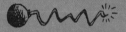

Teacher: Didn't you know the bell
had gone?
Silly Sue: I didn't take it, Miss.

Hil: Who was the fastest runner in history?
Bill: Adam. He was first in the human race.

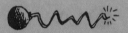

Did you hear about the teacher who was trying to instil good table manners in her girls? She told them, "A well-brought-up girl never crumbles her bread or rolls in her soup."

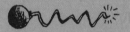

Did you hear about the boy who was told to do 100 lines? He drew 100 cats on the paper. He thought the teacher had said "lions."

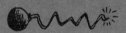

What's your handicrafts teacher like?
She's a sew and sew.

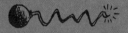

What gets bigger the more you take away?
A hole.

Why did the undertaker chop all his corpses into little bits? Because he liked them to rest in pieces.

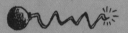

Why was the insect thrown out of the forest? Because he was a litter bug.

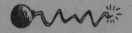

What did the undertaker say to his girlfriend? Em-balmy about you.

What happened when the pussy
swallowed a penny?
There was money in the kitty.

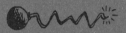

A young lad was helping his dad
with do-it-yourself jobs around
the house. "You know, son," said
the father, "you're just like
lightning with that hammer."
"Fast, eh?" said the boy.
"Oh, no – you never strike in the
same place twice."

What did the traffic light say to
the motorist?
Don't look now, I'm changing.

What's the difference between a
Peeping Tom and someone who's
just got out of the bath?
One is rude and nosey. The other
is nude and rosy.

Why did the lazy idiot apply for a
job in a bakery?
He fancied a long loaf.

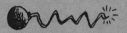

What's the difference between a
sigh, a car and a monkey?
A sigh is oh dear. A car is too dear.
A monkey is you, dear.

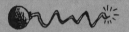

Was the carpenter's son a chip off
the old block?

Do you serve women in this bar?
No sir, you have to bring your own.

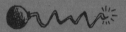

What happens if you play table
tennis with a bad egg?
First it goes ping, then it goes
pong.

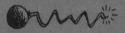

Who is Wyatt Burp?
The sheriff with the repeater.

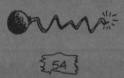

Why are school cooks cruel?
Because they batter fish and beat
eggs.

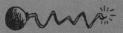

What's a giant's favorite tale?
A tall story.

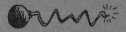

My sister thinks that a juggernaut
is an empty beer mug.

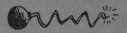

What did the Inuit children sing
when their principal was leaving?
Freeze a Jolly Good Fellow.

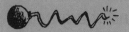

Ben's teacher regards Ben as a
wonder child. He wonders whether
he'll ever learn anything.

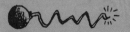

What do you get if you cross a
burglar with a concrete mixer?
A hardened criminal.

What's the difference between a crossword expert, a greedy boy and a pot of glue?
A crossword expert is a good puzzler and the greedy boy's a pud guzzler. The pot of glue? Ah, that's where you get stuck.

What's the difference between a kangaroo, a lumberjack and a bag of peanuts?

A kangaroo hops and chews and a lumberjack chops and hews.

Yes, but what's the bag of peanuts for?

For monkeys like you.

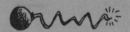

Who makes suits and eats spinach?

Popeye the Tailorman.

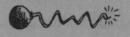

Where does Tarzan buy his
clothes?
At a Jungle Sale.

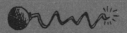

What kind of cans are there in
Mexico?
Mexicans.

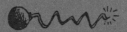

What is a mermaid?
A deep-she fish.

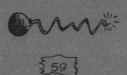

Is this a second-hand shop?
Yes, sir.
Good. Can you fit one on my
watch, please?

In the park this morning I was
surrounded by lions.
Lions! In the park?
Yes – dandelions!

Notice (in a new shop window):
Don't go elsewhere and be robbed
– try us!

Jennifer: Are you coming to my party?
Sandra: No, I ain't going.
Jennifer: Now, you know what Miss told us. Not ain't. It's I am not going, he is not going, she is not going, they are not going.
Sandra: Blimey, ain't nobody going?

A noise woke me up this morning.
What was that?
The crack of dawn.

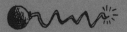

They're not going to grow bananas
any longer.
Really? Why not?
Because they're long enough
already.

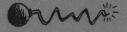

I wonder where I got that puncture?
Maybe it was at that last fork in the road . . .

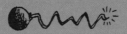

I bet I can make you speak like a Native American.
How?
That's right!

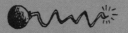

Passer-by (to fisherman): Is this river any good for fish?
Fisherman: It must be. I can't get any of them to leave it.

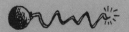

Why is perfume obedient?
Because it is scent wherever it goes.

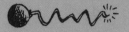

Which soldiers smell of salt and pepper?
Seasoned troops.

A man with a newt on his shoulder
walked into a pub. "What do you
call him?" asked the barmaid.
"Tiny," said the man.
"Why do you call him Tiny?"
"Because he's my newt!"

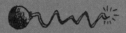

What do you get if you cross a nun
and a chicken?
A pecking order.

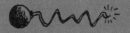

What does Luke Skywalker shave
with?
A laser blade.

Which capital city cheats at
exams?
Peking.

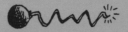

Why did the woman take a load of
hay to bed?
To feed her nightmare.

What happened when the wheel
was invented?
It caused a revolution.

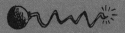

Ivan: What are you reading?
Andrea: It's a book about
electricity.
Ivan: Oh, current events?
Andrea: No, light reading.

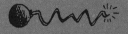

How did Benjamin Franklin
discover electricity?
It came to him in a flash.

Where do geologists go for
entertainment?
To rock concerts.

Why is history the sweetest
lesson?
Because it's full of dates.

What's wrong with this fish?
Long time, no sea.

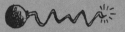

What did the tie say to the hat?
You go on ahead and I'll hang
around.

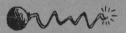

What did the picture say to the
wall?
I've got you covered.

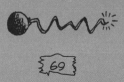

Why did the man take a pencil to bed?
To draw the curtains . . . I'd tell you another joke about a pencil, but it hasn't any point.

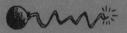

Why did the burglar take a shower?
He wanted to make a clean getaway.

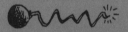

Why do idiots eat biscuits?
Because they're crackers.

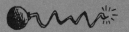

"What is your occupation?" asked
the magistrate.
"I'm a locksmith, your honor."
"And what were you doing in the
jeweler's shop at three in the
morning when the police officers
entered?"
"Making a bolt for the door!"

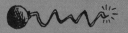

What do you call an American drawing?
Yankee Doodle.

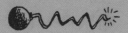

A stupid man was in court charged with parking his car in a restricted area. The judge asked if he had anything to say in his defense. "They shouldn't put up such misleading notices," said the stupid man. "It said FINE FOR PARKING HERE."

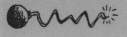

What do you call an American with a lavatory on his head?
John.

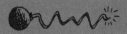

What's the name for a short-legged tramp?
A low-down bum.

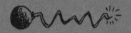

Why is it not safe to sleep on trains?
Because they run over sleepers.

Sign in a cafe: All drinking water in this establishment has been personally passed by the management.

Did you hear about the farmer's boy who hated the country?
He went to the big city and got a job as a shoe-shine boy, and so the farmer made hay while the son shone!

"Gosh, it's raining cats and dogs," said Suzie looking out of the kitchen window.

"I know," said her mother who had just come in. "I've just stepped in a poodle!"

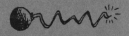

What did the Ancient Greeks shout when Archimedes fell in a dung-heap?

You Reeka! You Reeka!

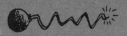

Classroom
Jokes

Alec turned up for football practice clutching a large broom.
"What's that for?" asked the coach.
"You said I was going to be sweeper today."

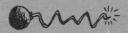

"Teacher is a bore!" was scrawled on the blackboard one day.
"I do not want to see that on my blackboard," he thundered when he saw it.
"Sorry, Sir! I didn't realize you wanted it kept secret."

"Ann! Point out Australia for me on the map."

Ann went to the front of the class, picked up the pointer and showed the rest of the class where Australia was.

"Well done! Now, Alec! Can you tell us who discovered Australia?"

"Er . . . Ann, Miss?"

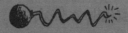

"And what might your name be?"
the school secretary asked the
new boy.
"Well it might be Cornelius, but it's
not. It's Sam."

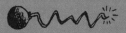

What happens if there's a collision
outside school?
There's usually a fight.

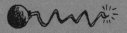

What happened to the baby chicken that misbehaved at school?
It was eggspelled.

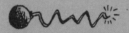

Teacher: I was going to read you a story called "The Invasion of the Body Snatchers," but I've changed my mind.
Class: Oh why, Miss?
Teacher: Because we might get carried away.

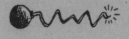

"Ann," said the dancing mistress.
"There are two things stopping you
becoming the world's greatest
ballerina."
"What are they, Miss?" asked
Ann.
"Your feet."

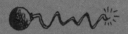

"I hope you're not one of those
boys who sits and watches the
school clock," said the principal to
a new boy.
"No, Sir. I've got a digital watch
that bleeps at half past three."

What's the definition of a school
report?
A poison pen letter from the
principal.

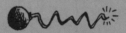

Why did the soccer teacher give
his team lighters?
Because they kept losing all their
matches.

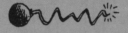

What's the difference between school dinners and a bucket of fresh manure?
School dinners are usually cold.

Did you hear about the cross-eyed teacher who had no control over her pupils?

What's the longest piece of furniture in the school?
The multiplication table.

What do you get if you cross old
potatoes with lumpy mince?
School dinners.

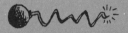

Miss Jones who teaches us maths,
Isn't a bundle of laughs.
For, sad to tell,
She doesn't half smell,
For she never takes any baths.

Did you hear about the teacher
who married the dairy maid?
It didn't last. They were like chalk
and cheese.

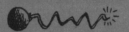

"Why are you crying Amanda?"
asked her teacher.
"'Cos Jenny's broken my new doll,
Miss," she cried.
"How did she do that?"
"I hit her on the head with it."

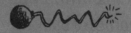

Did you hear about the teacher
who retired?
His class gave him an illuminated
address. They burned his house
down.

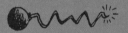

Confucius he say: If teacher ask
you question and you not know
answer, mumble.

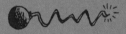

What did the arithmetic book say
to the geometry book?
Boy! Do we have our problems!

"And what's your name?" the secretary asked the next new boy.
"Butter."
"I hope your first name's not Roland," smirked the secretary.
"No, Miss. It's Brendan."

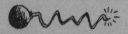

"What's your first name?" the teacher asked a new boy.
"It's Orson, Miss. I was named after Orson Welles, the film star."
"Just as well your last name's not Cart. Isn't it?"
"Yes Miss. It's Trapp."

A little girl was next in line. "My name's Curtain," she said.
"I hope your first name's not Annette?"
"No. It's Velvet."

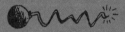

Did you hear about the math teacher who fainted in class? Everyone tried to bring her 2.

What's the difference between a boring teacher and a boring book? You can shut the book up.

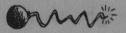

Teacher: That's the stupidest boy in the whole school.
Mother: That's my son.
Teacher: Oh! I'm so sorry.
Mother: You're sorry?

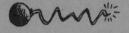

What has sixty feet and sings out of tune?
The school choir.

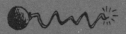

Typing teacher: Bob! Your work has certainly improved. There are only ten mistakes here.
Bob: Oh good, Miss.
Teacher: Now let's look at the second line, shall we?

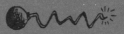

A teacher in a country school received the following letter from the mother of one of his students:

Dear Teacher,

Please excuse Phil from school last week. His father was ill and the pig had to be fed.

Yours sincerely,

Why are art galleries like retirement homes for teachers? Because they're both full of old masters.

It was sweltering hot outside. The teacher came into the classroom wiping his brow and said, "Ninety-two today. Ninety-two."
"Happy birthday to you. Happy birthday to you. . ." sang the class.

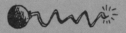

What makes a good librarian?
Shelf control.

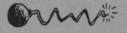

"What's your father's occupation?" asked the school secretary on the first day of the new term.

"He's a conjurer, Miss," said the new boy.

"How interesting. What's his favorite trick?"

"He saws people in half."

"Golly! Now next question. Any brothers and sisters?"

"One half-brother and two half-sisters."

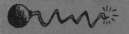

Billy's mother was called into the school one day by the principal. "We're very worried about Billy," he said. "He goes round all day 'cluck, cluck, clucking'."

"That's right," said Billy's mother. "He thinks he's a chicken."

"Haven't you taken him to a psychiatrist?"

"Well we would, but we need the eggs."

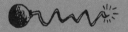

Two elderly teachers were talking over old times and saying how much things had changed. "I mean," said the first, "I caught one of the boys kissing one of the girls yesterday."

"Extraordinary," said the second. "I didn't even kiss my wife before I married her, did you?"

"I can't remember. What was her maiden name?"

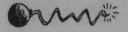

"Please Sir. There's something wrong with my stomach."
"Well button up your jacket and no one will notice."

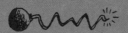

"Now remember boys and girls," said the science teacher. "You can tell a tree's age by counting the rings in a cross section. One ring for each year."
Alec went home for tea and found a Swiss Roll on the table.
"I'm not eating that, Mom," he said. "It's five years old."

Did you hear about the schoolboy
who just couldn't get to grips with
decimals?
He couldn't see the point.

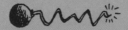

A warning to any young sinner,
Be you fat or perhaps even thinner.
If you do not repent,
To Hell you'll be sent.
With nothing to eat but school
dinner.

A mother was desperate to get her under-age daughter into kindergarten and was trying to impress the headmistress with the child's intellectual abilities. "She'll easily keep up with the others even though she is a year younger."

"Well," said the teacher doubtfully. "Could she prove it by saying something?"

"Certainly Miss," said the child. "Something pertaining to your conversation, or something purely irrelevant?"

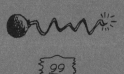

99

Why did the science teacher marry the school cleaner?
Because she swept him off his feet.

How do Religious Education
teachers mark exams?
With spirit levels.

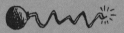

Teacher's strong; teacher's gentle.
Teacher's kind. And I am mental.

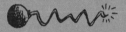

Please Sir! Please Sir! Why do you
keep me locked up in this cage?
Because you're the teacher's pet.

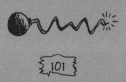

Teacher: Are you good at arithmetic?

Mary: Well, yes and no.

Teacher: What do you mean, yes and no?

Mary: Yes, I'm no good at arithmetic.

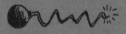

Why is a pencil the heaviest thing in your satchel?

Because it's full of lead.

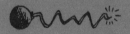

Mrs Jones: Well, Billy, how are you getting along with the trampolining in PE?

Billy: Oh, up and down, you know.

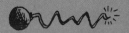

Mandy: Our teacher went on a special banana diet.

Andy: Did she lose weight?

Mandy: No, but she couldn't half climb trees well!

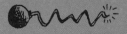

Art Teacher: What color would you paint the sun and the wind?
Brian: The sun rose, and the wind blue.

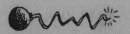

Teacher: Your books are a disgrace, Archibald. I don't see how anyone can possibly make as many mistakes in one day as you do.
Archibald: I get here early, Sir.

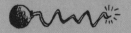

When is an English teacher like a judge?
When she hands out long sentences.

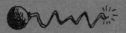

Geography Teacher: What mineral do we import from America?
Daft Darren: Coca-Cola!

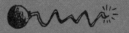

What's black and white and horrible?
A math exam paper.

What nickname did the police give to the new blonde woman police officer?
A fair cop.

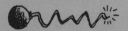

Kelly: Is God a doctor, Miss?
Teacher: In some ways, Kelly. Why do you ask?
Kelly: Because the Bible says that the Lord gave the tablets to Moses.

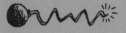

How can you tell when it's rabbit pie
for school dinner?
It has hares in it.

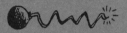

Can you spell a composition with
two letters?
SA (essay).

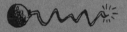

What did the pen say to the paper?
I dot an "i" on you.

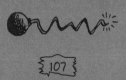

What is brown, hairy, wears dark glasses and carries a pile of exercise books?
A coconut disguised as a teacher.

Why did the teacher put corn in his shoes?
Because he had pigeon toes.

What do you call a deaf teacher?
Anything you like, he can't hear you.

How can a teacher double his money?
By folding it in half.

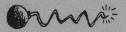

Teacher: What is a Native American's home called?
Andy: I don't know, Miss, but I know what a little Native American's joke is called.
Teacher: Well, what is it called?
Andy: A Minihaha.

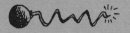

Girl: My teacher's a peach.
Mother: You mean she's sweet.
Girl: No, she has a heart of stone.

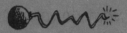

Headmaster: I've called you into
my office, Peter, because I want to
talk to you about two words I wish
you wouldn't use so often. One is
"great" and the other is "lousy."
Peter: Certainly Sir. What are they?

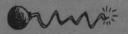

Mother: How was your first day at school?
Little Boy: OK, but I haven't got my present yet.
Mother: What do you mean?
Little Boy: Well the teacher gave me a chair, and said "Sit there for the present."

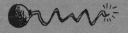

Teacher to pupil: How many thousand times have I told you not to exaggerate?

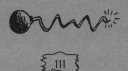

Father: Jennifer, I've had a letter from your principal. It seems you've been neglecting your appearance.

Jennifer: Dad?

Father: He says you haven't appeared in school all week.

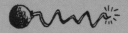

Teacher: What happened to your homework?

Boy: I made it into a paper plane and someone hijacked it.

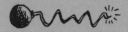

Tom: Why are you scratching your head?

Harry: I've got those arithmetic bugs again.

Tom: Arithmetic bugs – what are they?

Harry: Well, some people call them head lice.

Tom: Then why do you call them arithmetic bugs?

Harry: Because they add to my misery, subtract from my pleasure, divide my attention and multiply like crazy.

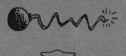

113

Teacher: What's the best way to pass this geometry test?
Boy: Knowing all the angles?

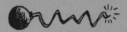

Teacher: You should have been here at nine o'clock.
Boy: Why? Did something happen?

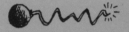

Mother: What did you learn at school today?
Son: Not enough. I have to go back tomorrow.

Teacher: If I had ten flies on my desk, and I swatted one, how many flies would be left?
Girl: One – the dead one!

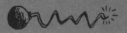

One unfortunate teacher started off a lesson with the following instruction, "I want you all to give me a list of the lower animals, starting with Georgina Clark . . ."

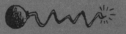

Music master: Brian, if "f" means forte, what does "ff" mean?
Brian: Eighty!

"Frank," said the weary math teacher, "if you had seven dollars in one pocket, and seven dollars in another pocket, what would you have?"
"Someone else's trousers on!"

Teacher: Martin, I've taught you everything I know, and you're still ignorant!

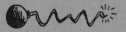

Teacher: Ford, you're late for school again. What is it this time?
Ford: I sprained my ankle, sir.
Teacher: That's a lame excuse.

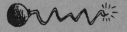

Cooler Cracks

Did you hear about the man who
drowned in a bowl of muesli?
A strong currant pulled him under.

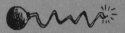

What holds the moon up?
Moon beams.

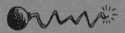

What kind of cats love water?
Octopuses.

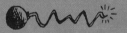

Bertie: My mom asked the doctor for something for wind.
Gertie: What did he do?
Bertie: He gave her a kite.

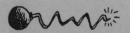

Kevin: I'm really cool, you know.
Kieran: I always thought you were a cold fish.

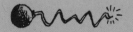

Why is a football stadium cool?
It's full of fans.

How do you know if your cat's got a bad cold?
He has cat-arrh.

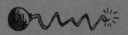

What do you give a pony with a cold?
Cough stirrup.

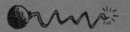

What does an octopus wear when it's cold?
A coat of arms.

What goes "hum-choo, hum-choo"?
A bee with a cold.

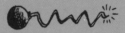

What's a cold, evil candle called?
The wicked wick of the north.

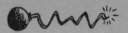

What kind of medicine does Dracula take for a cold?
Coffin medicine.

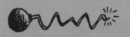

What happened to the zombie who had a bad cold?
He said, "I'm dead up wid fuddy jokes aboud zondies."

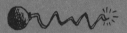

Werewolf: Doctor, doctor, thank you so much for curing me.
Doctor: So you don't think you're a werewolf anymore?
Werewolf: Absolutely not, I'm quite clear now – see my nose is nice and cold.

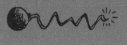

Doctor, doctor, what would you take
for this cold?
Make me an offer.

Why do skeletons hate winter?
Because the cold goes right
through them.

What kind of dance do cool people
hate?
A square dance.

Doctor, doctor, I keep thinking I'm a dog out in the cold.
Oh, stop whining.

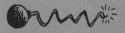

What happened when the ice monster had a furious row with the zombie?
He gave him the cold shoulder.

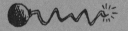

What goes into the water pink and comes out blue?
A swimmer on a cold day!

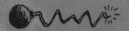

What's hairy and damp and sits shivering at fairs?
A coconut with a cold.

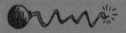

What's the difference between a bus driver and a cold?
One knows the stops; the other stops the nose.

Why can you run faster when you've got a cold?
Because you have a racing pulse and a running nose.

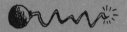

How many months have 28 days?
All of them.

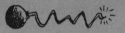

What season is it when you are on a trampoline?
Springtime.

Geography teacher: What is the coldest place in the world?
Ann: Chile.

What can a schoolboy keep and give away at the same time?
A cold.

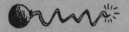

Did you hear about the snake with a bad cold?
No! Tell me about the snake with a bad cold.
She had to viper nose.

What is hairy and coughs?
A coconut with a cold.

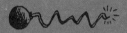

Teacher: Matthew, what is the
climate of New Zealand?
Matthew: Very cold, sir.
Teacher: Wrong.
Matthew: But sir! When they send
us meat, it always arrives frozen!

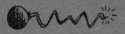

Lady (to a tramp who's asked for a meal): Do you like cold prunes and custard?

Tramp: I love it, lady.

Lady: Well, call back later, it is very hot right now.

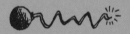

Young Horace was being taught how to box, but so far hadn't landed a single blow on his opponent.

"Don't worry, lad," said his teacher, "keep swinging – the draft might give him a cold."

It was raining, and the goalie had let several goals through. As he came off the pitch he sniffed, and said, "I think I've caught a cold." "I'm pleased to hear you can catch something," replied a fellow player.

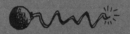

It was a warm day and the baseball player kept missing his shots. After the match he sighed and said, "What couldn't I do with a long, cold drink?"
"Hit it?" inquired a fellow player.

Billy: Is your cold better?
Tilly: I've got a very bad head but I hope to shake it off soon.

He's so cold-blooded that if a mosquito bit him it would get pneumonia.

You're like a summer cold!
What do you mean?
It's impossible to get rid of you!

What animal with two humps can be found at the North Pole?
A lost camel.

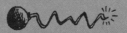

Neddy: I've got a cold in the head.
Teddy: It must be the first time you've had anything in your head.

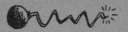

How do sheep keep warm in winter?
Central bleating.

What likes to spend the summer in a fur coat and the winter in a swimsuit?
A moth.

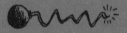

First cat: Where do fleas go in winter?
Second cat: Search me!

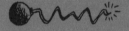

Waiter, waiter, there's a wasp in my pudding.
So that's where they go to in the winter.

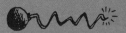

Why don't vultures fly south in the winter?
Because they can't afford the air fare.

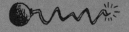

Teacher: Why do birds fly south in winter?
Jim: Because it's too far to walk.

Why did the canoeist take a water pistol with him?
So he could shoot the rapids.

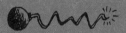

What's thick, black, floats on water and shouts "Knickers!"?
Crude oil.

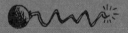

What do you get if you cross a bottle of water with an electric eel?
A bit of a shock really!

What insect can fly underwater?
A bluebottle in a submarine.

What happens if you upset a
cannibal?
You get into hot water.

What do you call a witch who likes
the beach but is scared of the
water?
A chicken sand-witch.

What's sweet, cold and hurtles up
the motorway on a stick?
An articulated lolly.

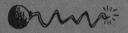

What do you call a man who
forgets to put his underpants on?
Nicholas.

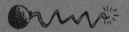

What do you call an alien starship
that drips water?
A crying saucer.

"Now don't forget boys," the science teacher droned on, "if it wasn't for water we would never learn to swim. And if we'd never learned to swim, just think how many people would have drowned!"

Did Adam and Eve ever have a date?
No, they had an apple.

Did you hear about the idiot who
made his chickens drink boiling
water?
He thought they would lay hard
boiled eggs.

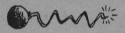

Teacher: Martin, put some more
water in the fish tank.
Martin: But, Sir, they haven't drunk
the water I gave them yesterday.

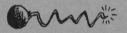

Mrs Twigg took her class on a nature ramble. They went past a large duck pond. "Be careful not to fall in, children," she said, "the water's very deep." "But it can't be, Miss," said Susie, "it only comes up to the middle of those ducks."

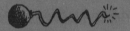

Why did the music student have a piano in the bathroom?
Because he was practicing Handel's Water Music.

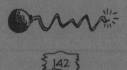

What is the loudest sport?
Tennis, because everyone raises a racquet (racket).

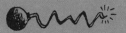

Anne: Ugh! The water in my glass is cloudy.
Dan, trying to impress his new girlfriend: It's alright, it's just the glass that hasn't been washed.

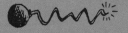

Daddy, daddy, can I have another glass of water please?

But that's the tenth one I've given you tonight.

Yes, but the baby's bedroom is still on fire.

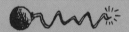

When is the water in the shower room musical?

When it's piping hot.

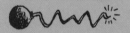

Why did the teacher wear a lifejacket at night?
Because she liked sleeping on a waterbed, and couldn't swim!

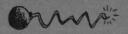

Which is the ghost's favorite stretch of water?
Lake Eerie.

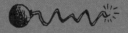

Did you hear about the stupid water-polo player?
His horse drowned . . .

What is full of holes but can hold water?
A sponge.

A man in a swimming pool was on the very top diving board. He poised, lifted his arms, and was about to dive when the attendant came running up, shouting, "Don't dive – there's no water in that pool!" "That's alright," said the man. "I can't swim!"

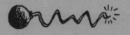

The food at the club dinner was awful. The soup tasted like dishwater, the fish was off, the meat was overcooked, and the vegetables were obviously old. The last straw for one member was the custard, which was thick and lumpy. "This meal is disgusting!" he roared. "And what's more, I'm going to bring it up at the AGM next week!"

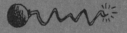

Policeman: Why are you driving with a bucket of water on the passenger seat?
Motorist: So I can dip my headlights.

Jane: Have you noticed that your mother smells a bit funny these days?
Wayne: No. Why?
Jane: Well your sister told me she was giving her a bottle of toilet water for her birthday.

What has a big mouth but doesn't
say a word?
A river.

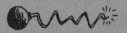

He's so dumb that after he'd
watched a gardening program on
TV he started watering the light
bulbs.

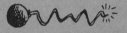

I hear he's a very careful person.
Well, he likes to economize on soap
and water.

What happened to the yacht that sank in shark-infested waters? It came back with a skeleton crew.

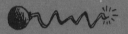

Why didn't the idiot go water-skiing when he was on holiday? He couldn't find a sloping lake.

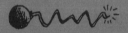

Notice by a river: When this sign is under water the towpath is flooded.

Mrs Green: How's your new house?
Mrs Brown: The roof needs mending. In last week's storm rain was coming down the walls like water.

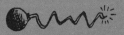

If we want to keep our heads above water we must keep our ears to the ground.

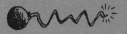

Bob: They say he has a waterproof voice.
Ted: What do you mean?
Bob: It can't be drowned out.

Ronnie: Why are you bathing in such dirty water?
Donnie: It wasn't dirty when I got in it.

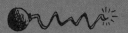

How can I cure water on the knee?
Wear pumps.

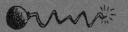

Why do watermelons have to have a formal wedding?
Because they can't-elope.

Why didn't the man believe what
the sardine said?
It sounded too fishy.

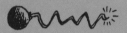

Why did the nature lover plant bird
seed?
He wanted to grow canaries.

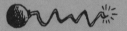

Why did the farmer plant old car
parts in his garden?
He wanted to raise a bumper crop.

Doctor: You need new glasses.
Monster: How did you guess?
Doctor: I could tell the moment you
walked through the window.

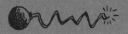

What do you get if you divide the
circumference of a pig by its
diameter?
Pork pi.

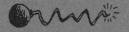

A wizard went to the doctor one day complaining of headaches. "It's because I live in the same room as two of my brothers," he said. "One of them has six goats and the other has four pigs and they all live in the room with us. The smell is terrible." "Well couldn't you just open the windows?" asked the doctor. "Certainly not," he replied, "my bats would fly out."

What helps keep your teeth
together?
Toothpaste.

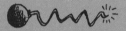

How did the teacher forecast the
weather with a piece of string?
She hung it up, and if it moved,
she knew it was windy, and if it got
wet, she knew it was raining.

Why does the Hound of the Baskervilles turn round and round before he lies down for the night? Because he's the watchdog and he has to wind himself up.

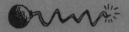

Doctor, doctor, I think I'm Napoleon. How long have you felt like this? Since Waterloo.

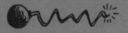

Mr Jones met a neighbor carrying
a front door. "Why are you carrying
that, Tom?" asked Mr Jones.
"I've lost my key," replied Tom.
"Oh," said Mr Jones, "so how will
you get in?"
"It's alright – I've left the window
open."

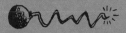

Who broke the window?
It was Andrew, Dad. He ducked
when I threw a stone at him.

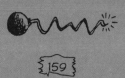

What insect is like the top of a
house?
A tick (attic).

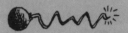

What is nothing but holes tied to
holes, yet is as strong as iron?
A chain.

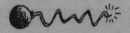

What is the best way to raise
strawberries?
With a spoon.

Sign in shop window: FOR SALE
Pedigree bulldog. Housebroken.
Eats anything. Very fond of
children.

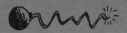

A man is in a prison cell with no
windows and no doors; there are
no holes in the ceiling or trapdoors
in the floor, yet in the morning the
wardens find him gone. How did
he get out?
Through the doorway – there were
no doors remember!

At a very posh wedding, one of the guests broke wind. The bridegroom was furious and rounded on the guilty party. "How dare you break wind in front of my wife?" he roared. "Sorry," said the guest. "Was it her turn?"

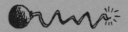

What is the correct thing to do before the King of Trees? Bough (bow).

Dad, there's a man at the door collecting for the new swimming pool.
Give him a glass of water!

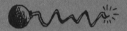

Who was the first underwater spy?
James Pond.

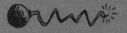

What happened when the bell fell in the water?
It got wringing wet.

Don't look out of the window,
Lavinia, people will think it's
Hallowe'en.

Dylan: I take lots of exercise.
Duncan: I thought so. That's why
you're so long-winded.

What happened to the man who
couldn't tell putty from custard?
His windows fell out.

What happened to the man who couldn't tell the difference between putty and porridge? His teeth stuck together and his windows fell out.

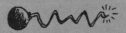

Father: George! Don't let the dog hang his head out of the window whilst driving!

Pungent Pongs

Did you hear the joke about the skunk?
Never mind, it stinks!

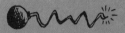

What do you get if you cross a skunk with a boomerang?
A bad smell you can't get rid of.

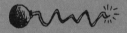

Scotty: I say, I say, I say, my dog's got no nose!
Snotty: How does he smell?
Scotty: Terrible!

What do you get if you cross a skunk with a porcupine?
A smelly pin cushion.

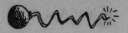

Did you hear about the dog that ate garlic?
His bark was worse than his bite.

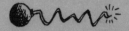

What did one sardine say to the other sardine when he saw a submarine?
"There goes a can full of people."

What do guests do at a cannibal
wedding?
They toast the bride and groom.

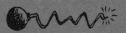

Why did the cannibal have a bad
stomach?
Because he ate people who
disagreed with him.

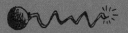

What did the vegetarian cannibal
eat?
Swedes.

What kind of girl does a mummy
take on a date?
Any old girl he can dig up.

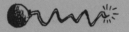

Why did the cannibal feel sick
after eating the missionary?
Because you can't keep a good
man down.

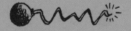

What kind of aftershave do
monsters wear?
Brute.

Did you hear about the plastic
surgeon?
He sat in front of the fire and
melted.

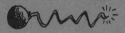

"I wouldn't say he was filthy, but
his clothes get dirtier on the
inside than on the outside."

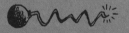

"Mommy, Mommy, why can't we
have a garbage bin?"
"Shut up and keep chewing."

I wouldn't say Basil was insensitive, but he did walk into a crematorium and ask what was cooking!

Stinker: I know a cafe where we can eat dirt cheap.
Pongo: But who wants to eat dirt?

Waiter: Soup's off today, sir.
Diner: I'll say it is. Mine had green mould on it.

What does a professor of anatomy
eat with cheese?
Pickled organs.

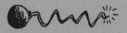

Why did the orchestra player live
on baked beans?
So he could play the Trumpet
Voluntary.

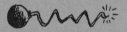

Did you hear the joke about the
three eggs?
Two bad.

What do you get if you cross a
pudding with a cow pat?
A smelly jelly.

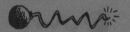

Knock Knock.
Who's there?
Kipper.
Kipper who?
Kipper your hands to yourself.

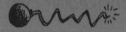

What's the dirtiest word in the
world?
Pollution.

What's brown and sounds like a
bell?
Dung.

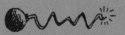

Mr Stench, peering over garden
fence: What are you going to do
with that pile of manure?
Mr Pong: Put it on my
strawberries.
Mr Stench: Really? I put cream on
mine.

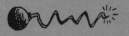

Why was the silly man expelled
from the committee meeting?
He passed the wrong sort of
motion.

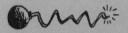

What has two legs, one wheel, and
stinks to high heaven?
A barrowload of manure.

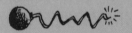

Did you hear about the posh school
where all the pupils smelled?
It was for filthy rich kids only.

Doctor: I can't diagnose the cause of your bad breath. I think it must be the drink.
Patient: OK, I'll come back when you're sober.

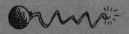

Did you hear about the man who had B.O. on one side only?
He bought Right Guard, but couldn't find any Left Guard.

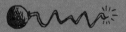

"Do you know," said the teacher to
one of her pupils who had B.O.,
"that we call you the wonder child
in the staffroom?"
"Why's that, Miss?"
"Because we all wonder when
you're going to wash!"

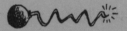

Doctor, doctor, these pills you gave
me for B.O. . . .
What's wrong with them?
They keep slipping from under my
arms!

Do you always talk like that or are you wearing itchy underwear?

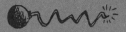

Knock Knock.
Who's there?
Underwear.
Underwear who?
Underwear my baby is tonight.

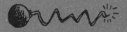

How can you spell too much with two letters?
XS (excess).

What disease makes you better at sport?
Athlete's foot.

What do you get if you cross a vampire with a rose?
A flower that goes for your throat when you sniff it.

What's yellow and sniffs?
A banana with a bad cold.

How many drops of acetic acid
does it take to make a stink bomb?
Quite a phew.

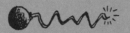

Did you hear about the little man
who thought he was Dracula?
He was a pain in the bum.

Why is a man wearing sunglasses
like a rotten teacher?
Because he keeps his pupils in the
dark.

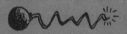

What has a bottom at the top?
I don't know.
Your legs.

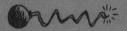

What comes out at night and goes
"Munch, munch, ouch"?
A vampire with a rotten tooth.

Chased by a Werewolf – by Claude
Bottom

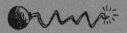

What do elephants wear under
their trousers?
Elepants.

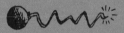

What is the best way to find a pin
in a rug?
Walk around in your bare feet.

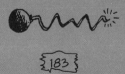

How do you stop a skunk from
smelling?
Fix a clothes peg to its nose.

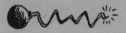

What's purple and hums?
A rotten plum!

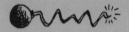

What has a head but no brain?
A cabbage.

What smells most in the zoo?
Your nose.

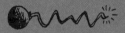

What is a bacteria?
The rear entrance of a cafeteria.

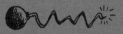

Why was the shoe unhappy?
Because his father was a loafer
and his mother was a sneaker.

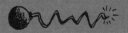

What's the difference between a skunk and a mouse?
A skunk uses a cheaper deodorant.

Why did the skunk buy six boxes of paper handkerchiefs?
Because he had a stinking cold.

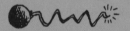

What did the skunk say when the wind changed from west to east?
"It's all coming back to me now."

What do you get if you cross a
young goat with a pig?
A dirty kid.

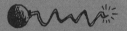

Why do giraffes have such long
necks?
Because their feet smell.

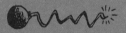

Why do people keep away from
bats?
Because of their bat breath.

Food and Physical Jokes

Jane's father decided to take all the family out to a restaurant for a meal. As he'd spent quite a lot of money for the meal he said to the waiter, "Could I have a bag to take the leftovers home for the dog?" "Gosh!" exclaimed Jane, "are we getting a dog?"

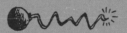

Why is it that when I stand on my head the blood rushes to my head but when I stand on my feet the blood doesn't rush to my feet? Your feet aren't empty.

A fat girl went into a cafe and ordered two slices of apple pie with four scoops of ice cream covered with lashings of raspberry sauce and piles of chopped nuts. "Would you like a cherry on the top?" asked the waitress.

"No, thanks," said the girl, "I'm on a diet."

Mom: Eat up your roast beef, it's full of iron.

Dottie: No wonder it's so tough.

A woman telephoned her local newspaper to let them know that she had just given birth to eighteen children. The reporter didn't quite hear the message and said, "Would you repeat that?"
"Not if I can help it," replied the woman.

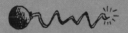

Neil: I've changed my mind.
Jim: About time, too. Does the new one work any better?

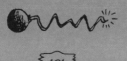

You should get a job in the
meteorology office.
Why?
Because you're an expert on wind.

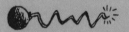

That boy is so dirty, the only time
he washes his ears is when he
eats watermelon.

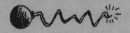

Waiter, how long have you worked
here?
Six months, Sir.
Well, it can't have been you who
took my order.

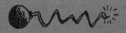

What happened to Lady Godiva's
horse when he realized that she
wasn't wearing any clothes?
It made him shy.

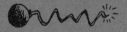

Doctor, doctor, I think I'm a spoon.
Sit over there, please, and don't
stir.

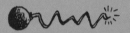

Doctor, doctor, my son's just
swallowed some gunpowder!
Well, don't point him at me.

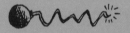

Doctor, doctor, I'm at death's door!
Don't worry, Mrs Jenkins. An
operation will soon pull you
through.

Doctor, doctor, Cuthbert keeps
biting his nails!
That's not serious in a child.
But Cuthbert bites his toenails.

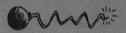

Doctor: Good morning, Mrs
Feather. Haven't seen you for a
long time.
Mrs Feather: I know, doctor. It's
because I've been ill.

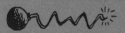

Why did the farmer plough his field with a steamroller?
Because he planned to grow mashed potatoes.

Doctor, I keep stealing things. What can I do?
Try to resist the temptation, but if you can't, get me a new television.

Nicky and Vicky were talking about a famous, very glamorous film star. "What do you think of her clothes?" asked Nicky. "I'd say they were chosen to bring out the bust in her," replied Vicky.

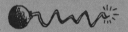

How did the baker get an electric shock? He stood on a bun and a current ran up his leg.

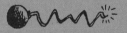

Did you hear about Lenny the Loafer? He is so lazy that he sticks his nose out of the window so that the wind will blow it for him.

Doctor, doctor, how can I stop my cold going to my chest?
Tie a knot in your neck.

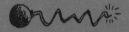

Doctor, doctor, I keep losing my memory.
When did you first notice that?
When did I first notice what?

Some people say the school cook's cooking is out of this world.
Most pupils wish it was out of their stomachs.

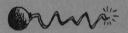

Waiter, waiter, why is my apple pie all mashed up?
You did ask me to step on it, Sir.

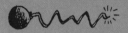

Do men always snore?
Only when they are asleep.

What did the dinner lady say when the teacher told her off for putting her finger in his soup?
It's alright, it isn't hot.

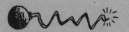

Brian: How did you manage to get a black eye?
Bertie: You see that tree in the playground?
Brian: Yes.
Bertie: Well, I didn't.

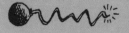

Waiter, waiter, have you got frogs' legs?
No Sir, I always walk like this.

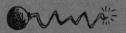

Ben, sniffing: Smells like UFO for dinner tonight, chaps.
Ken: What's UFO?
Ben: Unidentified Frying Objects.

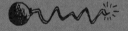

What tricks do eggs play on each other?
Practical yolks.

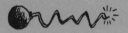

Doctor, doctor, my wife thinks she's a duck.
You better bring her in to see me straight away.
I can't do that – she's already flown south for the winter.

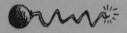

What kind of beans do cannibals
like best?
Human beans.

Doctor, doctor, I think I'm invisible.
Who said that?

Did you hear about the two fat
men who ran in the New York
Marathon?
One ran in short bursts, the other
in burst shorts!

Did you hear about the dentist
who became a brain surgeon?
His drill slipped.

What do traffic wardens like for tea?
Traffic jam sandwiches.

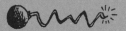

Cannibal Boy: I've brought a friend home for dinner.
Cannibal Mom: Put him in the fridge and we'll have him tomorrow.

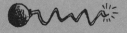

What is a dimple?
A pimple going the wrong way.

What happened to the man who put his false teeth in backwards?
He ate himself!

What is the most popular food served at a nudist camp?
Skinless sausages.

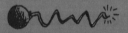

What's the best thing to put into a pizza?
Your teeth.

Ronald had broken a rib playing rugby. He went to the doctor, who asked how he was feeling. "I keep getting a stitch in my side," he replied.

"That's good," said the doctor. "It shows the bone is knitting."

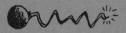

A man who tests people's eyes is called an optimist.

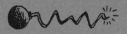

Why did the old lady cover her mouth with her hands when she sneezed?
To catch her false teeth.

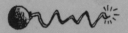

There was a fight in the fish shop last night – a whole lot of fish got battered!

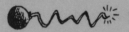

Doctor, doctor, I keep seeing double.
Take a seat, please.
Which one?

What kind of jokes does a chiropodist like?
Corny jokes.

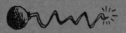

Doctor, doctor, I think I've been bitten by a vampire.
Drink this glass of water.
Will it make me better?
No, but I'll be able to see if your neck leaks.

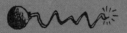

Which vegetable goes best with
jacket potatoes?
Button mushrooms.

How can you tell an old person
from a young person?
An old person can sing and brush
their teeth at the same time.

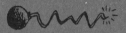

My auntie has a sore throat. What
should she do?
Take aunti-septic.

Who's stronger than a muscleman
who can tear up a telephone
directory?
Someone who can tear up a street.

Ben's new girlfriend uses such greasy lipstick that he has to sprinkle his face with sand to get a better grip.

Waiter: And how did you find your meat, Sir?
Customer: Oh, I just lifted a potato and there it was.

Why are fried onions like a photocopying machine?
They keep repeating themselves.

What happens if you tell a psychiatrist you are schizophrenic? He charges you double.

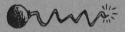

The kidneys are infernal organs.

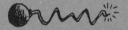

Doctor, doctor, it's wonderful! I feel like my old self again.
In that case we'd better start a new course of treatment.

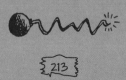

Doctor, doctor, I've only got fifty
seconds to live.
Just sit over there a minute.

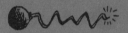

Did you hear about the girl who
got engaged to a chap and then
found out he had a wooden leg?
She broke it off, of course . . .

Why did the orange stop rolling
down the hill?
It ran out of juice.

My uncle's got a wooden leg. That's nothing. My auntie has a wooden chest.

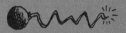

How do you make gold soup? Use fourteen carats.

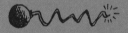

Waiter, waiter, there's a bird in my soup.
That's alright, Sir. It's bird-nest soup.

Waiter, waiter, this coffee tastes like mud.
I'm not surprised, Sir, it was ground only a few minutes ago.

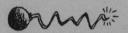

"I'm sorry," said the surgeon. "But I left a sponge in you when I operated last week."
"Oh," said the patient, "I was wondering why I was so thirsty all the time."

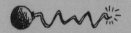

"Ugh! You smell terrible," said a doctor to a patient.

"That's odd," said the patient, "that's what the other doctor said."

"If you were told that by another doctor, why have you come to me?"

"Because I wanted a second opinion."

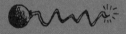

Trevor came rushing in to his dad. "Dad," he puffed, "is it true that an apple a day keeps the doctor away?"

"That's what they say," said his dad.

"Well, give us an apple quick — I've just broken the doctor's window!"

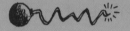

Jimmy was caught by his mother in the pantry. "And what do you think you're up to?" she asked furiously.

"I'm up to my seventh jelly tart," said Jimmy.

Now then, Deirdre, eat up all your greens like a good girl. They're good for your complexion, you know.

But I don't want to have a green complexion.

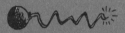

A tramp knocked on the back door of a house and asked for a bite to eat.

"Go away," said the lady of the house, "I never feed tramps."

"That's alright lady," said the tramp, "I'll feed myself."

"The trouble is," said the entertainer to the psychiatrist, "that I can't sing; I can't dance; I can't tell jokes; I can't act; I can't play an instrument or juggle or do magic tricks or do anything!"
"Then why don't you give up show-business?"
"I can't – I'm a star!"

Doctor, doctor, I'm becoming invisible!
Yes, I can see you're not all there.

A man sat on a train chewing gum and staring vacantly into space, when suddenly an old woman sitting opposite said, "It's no good you talking to me, young man, I'm stone deaf!"

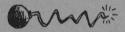

Doctor, doctor, you've taken out my tonsils, my adenoids, my gall-bladder, my varicose veins and my appendix, but I still don't feel well. That's quite enough out of you.

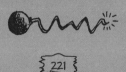

Little Jackie's mother was on the telephone to the boy's dentist. "I don't understand it," she complained, "I thought his treatment would only cost me $10, but you've charged me $40." "It is usually $10, madam," agreed the dentist, "but Jackie yelled so loudly that three of my other patients ran away!"

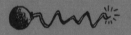

Three men were in the dock, and the judge, who had a terrible squint, said to the first, "How do you plead?"

"Not guilty," said the second.

"I'm not talking to you," snapped the judge.

"I didn't say a word," said the third.

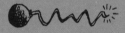

Summer Sensations

Where does an elephant go on
holiday?
Tuscany.

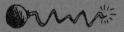

What do you call a mosquito on
holiday?
An itch-hiker.

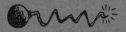

What do you say to a hitch-hiking
frog?
"Hop in!"

What do you get if you cross a frog
with a ferry?
A hoppercraft.

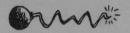

What do you get if you cross a
toadstool with a suitcase?
Not mushroom for your holiday
clothes.

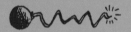

Which Cornish town is the favorite
holiday spot for rodents?
Mousehole.

What do bees do if they want to
use public transport?
Wait at a buzz stop.

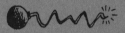

What happened when the cannibal
crossed the Atlantic on the QE2?
He told the waiter to take the
menu away and bring him the
passenger list.

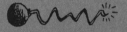

Where do witches go for their
holidays?
Bat-lins.

Why did the golfer wear two pairs
of trousers?
In case he got a hole in one.

How does the moon cut the sun's
hair?
Eclipse it.

Where do zombies go for cruises?
The Deaditerranean.

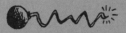

What do demons have on holiday?
A devil of a time.

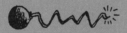

Where do ghosts go on holiday?
The Ghosta Brava.

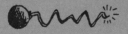

Where do ghost trains stop?
At devil crossings.

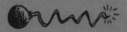

Why are ghosts at their loudest in
August?
Because they're on their
howlidays.

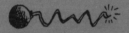

Which airway do ghouls fly with?
British Scareways.

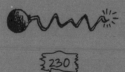

Where do ghosts like to go on holiday?
Goole.

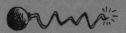

How did the rabbit get to Australia?
He flew by hareplane.

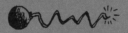

James: Do you know what nice people do on holiday?
John: No.
James: I didn't think you would.

Why couldn't the skeleton pay his bus fare?
Because he was skint.

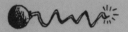

Why did the bat miss the bus?
Because he hung around too long.

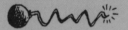

Why do you have to wait so long for a ghost train to come along?
They only run a skeleton service.

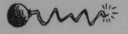

1st ghost: I died at Waterloo, you know.
2nd ghost: Really? Which platform?

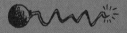

What can fall thousands of feet onto iron railings and not get hurt? A plane's shadow.

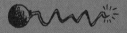

Which great Arab invented crisps? Sultan Vinegar.

Did you hear about the ghost who learned to fly?
He was pleased to be back on terror-firma.

What is the best time of the year to dig up carrots?
When the farmer is on holiday.

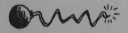

What happened when two televisions got married?
It was an awful wedding but the reception was great.

What steps should you take if you see a dangerous yeti on your travels?
Very large ones.

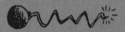

What do Paddington Bear and Winnie the Pooh pack for their holidays?
The bear essentials.

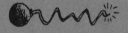

The seaside resort we went to last year was so boring that one day the tide went out and never came back.

How did the giant destroy three countries when he was on holiday? He picked up Turkey, dunked it in Greece and fried it in Japan.

Boss: You're looking much better now, Reynolds. How's that pain?
Reynolds: She's away on a business trip.

Charlie was very nervous about going in a plane. "Do these planes crash often?" he asked the flight attendant. "No," she smiled, "only once."

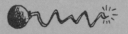

Nellie: Our form mistress went to the West Indies for her holidays.
Kelly: Jamaica?
Nellie: No, she went of her own accord.

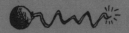

What can you see from the top of the Eiffel Tower?
Quite an eyeful!

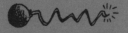

Which American city would a cow
like to visit?
Moo York.

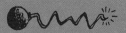

Crossing the Atlantic in a Rowing
Boat – by Eva Lott

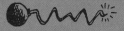

Summertime – by Theresa Greene

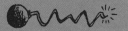

Sarah: I'm going to sunbathe on my holiday. I love the sun.

Susie: Oh, so do I. I could lie in the sun all day and all night.

Darren went on a camping holiday with his family. "Did the tent leak?" asked his friend Sharon. "Only when it rained," answered Darren.

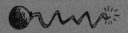

What did the sea say to the beach?
Nothing, it just waved.

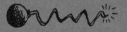

Why did the principal like to take her main holiday in the spring? She liked clean sheets on her bed.

Lizzie got a bad case of sunburn. When she complained how sore it was, her brother remarked, "Well, I guess you basked for it."

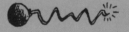

Passenger: Does this bus go to London?
Bus driver: No.
Passenger: But it says London on the front.
Bus driver: It says fish fingers on the side but we don't sell them!

In the summer holidays the math teacher collected information for a national opinion poll. But after a week she was sacked. Her vital statistics were wrong.

Why did the hotel manager ask
the talkative chess players to leave
his hotel?
Because he didn't like chess nuts
boasting in an open foyer.

Why was the man with a
photographic memory so unhappy?
He kept having negative thoughts.

What did the man with two left
feet wear to the beach?
Flip-flips.

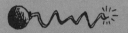

What do you call coconut trees
that exercise a lot?
Sweaty palms.

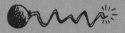

What stays hot in the fridge?
Chilli sauce.

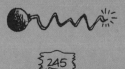

After years of traveling around the world, the wicked Abanazar finally discovered the enchanted cave in which he believed lay the magic lamp which would make him millions. He stood before the boulders which sealed the cave, and uttered the magic words, "Open, sesame!" There was a silence, and then a ghastly voice from within moaned, "Open says-a-who?"

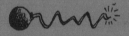

Why did the stupid pilot land his plane on a house?
Because the landing lights were on.

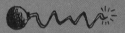

What makes the Tower of Pisa lean?
It doesn't eat much.

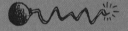

Why was the musician arrested?
He was always getting into treble.

Harry was telling his friend about his holiday in Switzerland. His friend had never been to Switzerland, and asked, "What did you think of the scenery?" "Oh, I couldn't see much," Harry admitted. "There were all those mountains in the way."

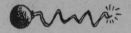

What's green, has four legs and two trunks?
Two seasick tourists.

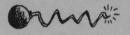

"Why did you come back early from your holidays?" one of Alec's friends asked him. "Well, on the first day we were there one of the chickens died and that night we had chicken soup. The next day one of the pigs died and we had pork chops . . ." "But why did you come back?" "Well, on the third day the farmer's father-in-law died. What would you have done?"

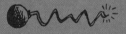

A woman just back from the United States was telling her friends about the trip. "When my husband first saw the Grand Canyon, his face dropped a mile," she said. "Why, was he disappointed with the view?" "No, he fell over the edge."

What is the best thing to take into the desert?
A thirst-aid kit.

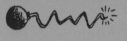

A new porter at a Paris hotel was instructed by the manager that it was important to call the guests by their names, in order to make them feel welcome and that the easiest way to find out their name was to look at their luggage. Armed with this advice, the porter took two guests up to their rooms, put down their bags and said, "I 'ope you 'ave a very 'appy stay 'ere in Paris, Mr and Mrs Genuine Cow'ide."

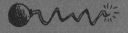

What do you think of this suit? I
had it made in Hong Kong.
Very nice, but what's that hump on
the back?
Oh, that's the tailor. He's still
working on it.

"I hope this plane doesn't travel
faster than sound," said the old
lady to a flight attendant. "Why?"
"Because my friend and I want to
talk, that's why."

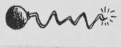

Last time my wife and I traveled on
the ferry from Newhaven to
Dieppe, we had six meals.
Six meals for that short crossing?
Three down and three up.

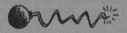

How do Spanish musicians catch
fish?
They castanet.

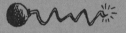

The transatlantic liner was experiencing particularly heavy weather, and Mrs Ramsbottom wasn't feeling well. "Would you care for some more supper, madam?" asked the steward. "No thanks," replied the wretched passenger. "Just throw it overboard to save me the trouble."

First explorer: There's one thing about Jenkinson.

Second explorer: What's that?

First explorer: He could go to headhunters' country without any fear – they'd have no interest in him.

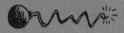

Why do oranges wear sun block?
Because they peel.

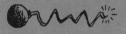

What is red outside, green and hairy inside, and very crowded?
A bus full of gooseberries.

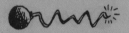

What's green and hairy and wears sunglasses?
A gooseberry on holiday.

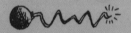

What's sweet, sour, dangerous and travels?
Takeaway Kung food.

Where's a shark's favorite holiday destination?
Finland.

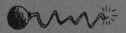

How do nits go on holidays?
British Hairways.

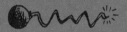

Why won't midfield players travel by airplane?
In case they are put on the wing.

What's red and wobbles on top of sponge cake and custard in the middle of Paris?
The Trifle Tower.

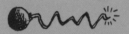

Kylie and Riley were talking about their forthcoming summer holidays. "Last year," said Kylie, "my brother and I took turns to bury each other in the sand." "Yes, but what about this year?" interrupted Riley. "I was coming to that," said Kylie. "This year we're going back to try to find him."

Local: Are you lost?
Stranger: No, I'm here. It's the bus station that's lost.

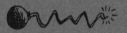

Letter from a travel agent: The flight you requested is fully booked but if someone falls out we'll let you know.

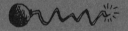

Notice at a railroad station: These toilets are out of order. Please use platform 6.

Louise: Did you hear about the stupid hitch-hiker?

Liza: No, what did he do?

Louise: He started his journey early so there wouldn't be so much traffic about.

Older brother: When I was a sailor I sailed both ways across the Atlantic without taking a bath.

Younger brother: I always said you were a dirty double crosser!

My Uncle Ben and Aunt Flo
haven't had a row for five years.
That's wonderful.
Not really. Uncle Ben lives in
China.

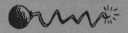

What happens when a plane runs
out of fuel?
All the passengers get out to push.

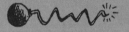

Just Plain Smelly

Two little girls were paddling on the beach. Nicky said, "Coo! Aren't your feet mucky?"

Sticky looked down at her feet. "They are a bit," she replied, "but you see, we didn't come last year."

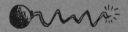

What do you call a dirty, frayed, hairy, blood-stained thing found on the bathroom floor?
A used Elastoplast.

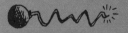

What does dirty rain do?
It showers.

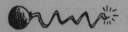

What do you call a woman with
egg, beans and chips on her
head?
Caff.

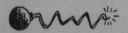

What does the Queen do when
she belches?
Issues a royal pardon.

Knock Knock.
Who's there?
Why?
Why who?
Why pa your nose, it's dripping.

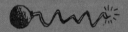

Knock Knock.
Who's there.
Few.
Few who?
Phew! There's an awful smell
round here, is it you?

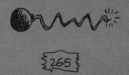

What do naughty cats leave
behind after a picnic?
Kitty litter.

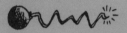

Who is the smelliest, hairiest
monarch in the world?
King Pong.

How do vampires keep their breath
smelling nice?
They use extractor fangs.

What do you give elephants with
big feet?
Big shoes.

Did you hear about the man who fell into a vat of curry?
He slipped into a korma.

First Witch: What's your new boyfriend like?
Second Witch: He's mean, nasty, ugly, smelly, and totally evil – but he has some bad points too.

Did you hear about the stupid man
who thought that "the great smell
of Brut" was King Kong's B.O.?

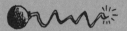

Doctor, doctor, I've got bad teeth,
foul breath and smelly feet.
Sounds like you've got foot and
mouth disease.

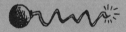

What do you get if you cross a
tarantula with a rose?
I don't know but I wouldn't try
smelling one.

Why are chickens so disgusting?
Because they're fowl.

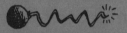

What has four legs, no sense of
humour and flies?
A dead hyena.

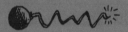

What do you get if you cross a
horse with a skunk?
Whinny the Pooh.

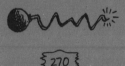

What happens if you give your
mouse some smelly cheese?
You make an awful mess of your
computer.

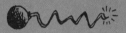

"Mary," said her teacher, "you
can't bring that lamb into school.
What about the smell?"
"Oh, that's alright Miss," said
Mary. "It'll soon get used to it."

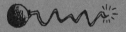

How do skunks find their way home?
Instinkt.

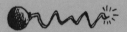

Did you hear about the horrible, hairy monster who did farmyard impressions?
He didn't do the noises, he just made the smells.

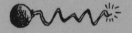

What do you get if you cross a skunk and an owl?
A bird that smells but doesn't give a hoot!

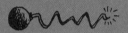

"What's your new perfume called?" a young man asked his girlfriend.
"High Heaven," she replied.
"I asked what it was called, not what it smells to!"

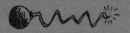

What kind of dog likes to take bubble baths?
A shampoodle.

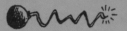

"There's a dreadful smell of B.O. in here," said the new office boy.
"It's the automatic air conditioning," said his boss.
"Automatic air conditioning?"
"Whenever the weather gets hot it automatically breaks down!"

A man with B.O. walked into a
drugstore and said, "I'd like
something to take this smell
away."
"So would I, Sir" said the druggist.
"So would I."

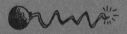

Did you hear about the new prize
for people who cure themselves of
B.O.?
It's called the No-Smell Prize.

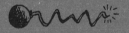

What dog smells of onions?
A hot dog.

What do you get if you cross a pig
with a laundry?
Hogwash.

What do you do if your nose goes
on strike?
Picket.

Doctor, doctor, my friend told me I had B.O.
And what makes you think he's right, you disgusting, smelly, malodorous, foul, little man?

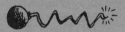

Why do the French never eat two eggs for breakfast?
Because one egg is un oeuf.

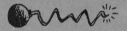

What's wet, smells and goes ba-bump, ba-bump?
A skunk in the spin-drier.

How is a telephone like a dirty
bathtub?
They both have rings.

Knock Knock.
Who's there?
Sonia.
Sonia who?
Sonia shoe. I can smell it from
here.

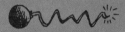

Why couldn't the skunk use her
phone?
It was out of odour.

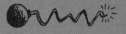

"Keep that dog out of my garden.
It smells disgusting!" a neighbor
said to a small boy one day.
The boy went home to tell everyone
to stay away from the neighbor's
garden because of the smell!

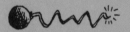

Have you heard about the new
aftershave that drives women
crazy?
No! Tell me about it.
It smells of fifty-dollar notes.

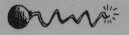

If a skunk wrote a book, which list
would it be on?
The top ten best smellers.

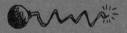

What smells of fish and goes
round and round at 100 miles an
hour?
A goldfish in a blender.

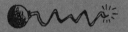

Doctor, doctor, my husband smells
like a fish.
Poor sole!

Doctor, doctor, I've had tummy ache since I ate three crabs yesterday.
Did they smell bad when you took them out of their shells?
What do you mean "took them out of their shells"?

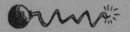

How can you tell if an elephant has been sleeping in your bed?
The sheets are wrinkled and the bed smells of peanuts.

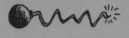

Knock Knock.
Who's there?
Hali.
Hali who?
Halitosis – your breath smells
awful!

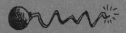

Darren: I'm so tired I feel like an
old sock.
Sharon: I thought there was a
funny smell in here!

Numbskulls

Why is the stupid red-headed boy like a biscuit?
Because he's a ginger nut.

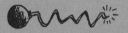

"How do you keep a stupid person happy for hours?"
"Give him a piece of paper with PTO written on both sides."

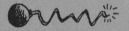

Did you hear about the man who hijacked a submarine? He demanded a million dollars and a parachute.

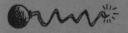

When he received the end-of-term report, Brenda's father went crazy. "This report is terrible," he said, "I'm not at all pleased with it." "I told the teacher you wouldn't like it," said Brenda, "but he insisted on sending it just the same."

A stupid glazier was examining a broken window. He looked at it for a while and then said: "It's worse than I thought. It's broken on both sides."

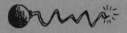

What are you if you step into a cow pat?
An incowpoop.

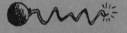

Why did the robot act stupid?
Because he had a screw loose.

My mother is so stupid that she
thinks a string quartet is four
people playing tennis.

A man telephoned London Airport.
"How long does it take to get to
New York?"
"Just a minute."
"Thanks very much."

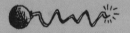

My friend is so stupid that he
thinks twice before saying nothing.

Why did the stupid sailor grab a bar of soap when his ship sank?
He thought he could wash himself ashore.

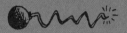

Did you hear about the sailor that was discharged from
the submarine service?
He was caught sleeping with the windows open.

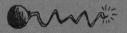

An idiotic laborer was told by an equally idiotic foreman to dig a hole in the road.

"And what shall I do with the earth, sir?" asked the laborer.

"Don't be daft, man," he replied. "Just dig another hole and bury it."

Did you hear about the stupid motorist who always drove his car in reverse?

It was because he knew the Highway Code backwards.

A stupid bank robber rushed into a bank, pointed two fingers at the clerk and said: "This is a muck up."

"Don't you mean a stick up?" asked the girl.

"No," said the robber, "it's a muck up. I've forgotten my gun."

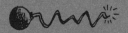

How do you confuse an idiot? Give him two spades and ask him to take his pick.

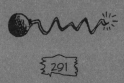

A stupid man spent the evening with some friends, but when the time came for him to leave, a terrific storm started with thunder, lightning and torrential rain. "You can't go home in this," said the host, "you'd better stay the night." "That's very kind of you," said the man, "I'll just pop home and get my pajamas."

A mountaineer fell down a very deep crevasse, breaking both his arms. Another member of the party managed to lower a rope until it was just within reach of the man's head.

"Quick!" he shouted. "Get hold of the rope with your teeth and I'll pull you up." Inch by painful inch, the mountaineer was dragged back up the crevasse. When he only had two feet to go, his rescuer called out, "Are you alright?"

"Yes, aaaaaaaaarrrrrrrgggggghhh hhhh!" came the reply.

Doctor: And did you drink your medicine after your bath, Mrs Soap?

Mrs Soap: No, doctor. By the time I'd drunk the bath there wasn't room for medicine.

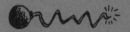

Waiter, waiter, this lobster's only got one claw.

It must have been in a fight, sir.

Then bring me the winner.

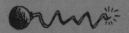

My sister is so stupid she thinks
that aroma is someone who travels
a lot.

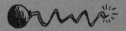

Did you hear about the idiot who
won the Tour de France?
He did a lap of honor.

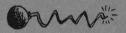

My friend is so stupid he thinks
that an autograph is a chart
showing sales figures for cars.

An idiot decided to start a chicken farm so he bought a hundred chickens to start. A month later he returned to the dealer for another hundred chickens because all of the first lot had died. A month later he was back at the dealers for another hundred chickens for the second lot had also died. "But I think I know where I'm going wrong," said the idiot. "I think I'm planting them too deep."

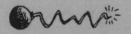

Why did the idiots' tug o' war
team lose the match?
They pushed.

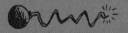

My big brother is such an idiot.
The other day I saw him hitting
himself on the head with a
hammer. He was trying to make
his head swell so his hat wouldn't
fall over his eyes.

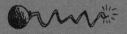

My sister is so dumb, she thinks that a buttress is a female goat.

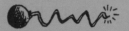

How does an idiot call for his dog? He puts two fingers in his mouth and then shouts Rover.

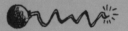

Did you hear about the idiotic karate champion who joined the army?
The first time he saluted, he nearly killed himself.

Sandra's mother said no young man in his right mind would take her to the school dance in her bikini, so she decided to go with her friend's stupid brother.

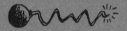

Teacher: You weren't at school last Friday, Robert. I heard you were out playing football.
Robert: That's not true, Sir. And I've got the cinema tickets to prove it.

Did you hear about the utterly brainless monster who sat on the floor?
He fell off.

Did you hear about the idiot who had a new bath put in? The plumber said, "Would you like a plug for it?"
The idiot replied, "Oh, I didn't know it was electric."

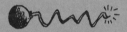

Wally Woollynut was given the job of painting a flagpole but he didn't know how much paint he would need. "Lay it down and measure it," suggested a mate.
"That's no good," said Wally, "I need to know the height, not the length."

Did you hear what Dumb Donald
did when he offered to paint the
garage for his Dad in the summer
holidays?
The instructions said "put on three
coats," so he went in and put on
his blazer, his raincoat and his
duffel coat.

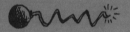

What's red, runs on wheels and
eats grass?
A bus. I lied about the grass.

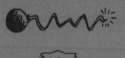

The math teacher and the English teacher went out for a quick pizza after school. "How long will the pizzas be?" asked the math teacher.

"Sorry, Sir," replied the waiter, "we don't do long pizzas, just ordinary round ones."

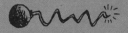

Wilberforce Witherspoon saw a notice outside a police station which read: MAN WANTED FOR ROBBERY. So he went in and applied for the job!

Simple Simon was writing a geography essay. It began, "The people who live in Paris are called parasites..."

My dad is stupid. He thinks a fjord is a Norwegian motor car.

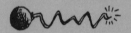

Jimmy, how many more times must I tell you to come away from that biscuit barrel?
No more, mom. It's empty.

Did you hear about the stupid photographer?
He saved burned-out light bulbs for use in his darkroom.

Why are orchestras so badly behaved?
They don't know how to conduct themselves.

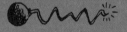

I can't understand the critics saying that only an idiot would like that television program. I really enjoyed it.

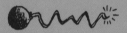

Father: Would you like a pocket calculator for Christmas, son?
Danny: No thanks, Dad. I know how many pockets I've got.

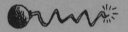

What did the football fan get when he listened to the match?
A burnt ear.

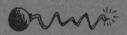

At the scene of a bank raid the police sergeant came running up to his inspector and said, "He got away, sir!"
The inspector was furious. "But I told you to put a man on all the exits!" he roared. "How could he have got away?"
"He left by one of the entrances, sir!"

A stupid man was struggling out of his house with a big table. His neighbor said to him, "Hello, Harry. Where are you going with that then?"

And Harry replied, "I'm taking it to the draper's shop to have it measured for a new tablecloth."

On their first evening in their new home the bride went in to the kitchen to fix a drink for her husband. Five minutes later she came back into the living room in tears.

"What's the matter, my angel?" asked her husband anxiously.

"Oh Derek!" she sobbed, "I put the ice cubes in hot water to wash them and now they've disappeared!"

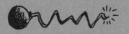

A doctor had been attending a rich old man for some time, but it became apparent that the old chap had not long to live. Accordingly, the doctor advised his wealthy patient to put his affairs in order. "Oh yes, I've done that," said the old gentleman. "I've only got to make my will. And do you know what I'm going to do with all my money? I'm going to leave it to the doctor who saves my life . . ."

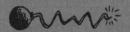

Vincent, why have you got a
sausage stuck behind your ear?
Eh? Oh no, I must have eaten my
pencil for lunch!

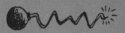

A man rushed into the doctor's
surgery, jumped on the doctor's
back, and started screaming
"One! Two! Three! Four!"
"Wait a minute!" yelled the doctor,
struggling to free himself. "What
do you think you're doing?"
"Well, doctor," said the eccentric
man, "they did say I could count on
you!"

The criminal mastermind found one of his gang sawing the legs off his bed. "What are you doing that for?" demanded the crook boss.

"Only doing what you ordered," said the stupid thug. "You told me to lie low for a bit!"

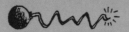

Did you hear about the man who tried to cross the Atlantic on a plank of wood?
He couldn't find a plank long enough.

A jeweler standing behind the counter of his shop was astounded to see a man come hurtling head-first through the window.

"What on earth are you up to?" he demanded.

"I'm terribly sorry," said the man, "I forgot to let go of the brick!"

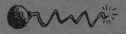

John kept pestering his parents to buy a video, but they said they couldn't afford one. So one day John came home clutching a package containing a brand-new video. "Wherever did you get the money to pay for that?" asked his father suspiciously.

"It's alright, Dad," replied John, "I traded the TV in for it."

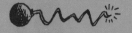

Nutty Knock Knock Jokes

Knock Knock.
Who's there?
Abba.
Abba who?
Abba'out turn!
Quick march!

Knock Knock.
Who's there?
Abel.
Abel who?
Abel to see you, ha, ha!

Knock Knock.
Who's there?
Adam.
Adam who?
Adam will burst any minute now.

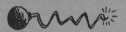

Knock Knock.
Who's there?
Adder.
Adder who?
Adder you get in here?

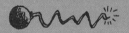

Knock Knock.
Who's there?
Ahmed.
Ahmed who?
Ahmed a big mistake coming here!

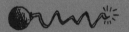

Knock Knock.
Who's there?
Aida.
Aida who?
Aida whole box of chocolates and I
feel really sick.

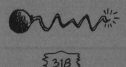

Knock Knock.
Who's there?
Quacker.
Quacker who?
Quacker 'nother bad joke and I'm
leaving.

Knock Knock.
Who's there?
Buster.
Buster who?
Buster blood vessel.

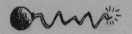

Knock Knock.
Who's there?
Butcher.
Butcher who?
Butcher left leg in, your left leg
out . . .

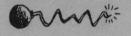

Knock Knock.
Who's there?
Butter.
Butter who?
Butter wrap up – it's cold out here.

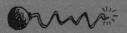

Knock Knock.
Who's there?
Caesar.
Caesar who?
Caesar arm to stop her getting
away.

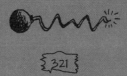

Knock Knock.
Who's there?
Canoe.
Canoe who?
Canoe lend me some money?

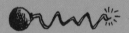

Knock Knock.
Who's there?
Canon.
Canon who?
Canon open the door then.

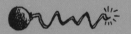

Knock Knock.
Who's there?
Card.
Card who?
Card you see it's me!

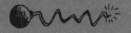

Knock Knock.
Who's there?
Carlo.
Carlo who?
Carload of junk.

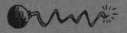

Knock Knock.
Who's there?
Delhi.
Delhi who?
Delhi a joke . . .

Knock Knock.
Who's there?
Delta.
Delta who?
Delta great hand of cards.

Knock Knock.
Who's there?
Denial.
Denial who?
Denial flows through Egypt.

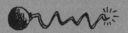

Knock Knock.
Who's there?
Denmark.
Denmark who?
Denmark your own territory.

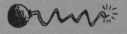

Knock Knock.
Who's there?
Depp.
Depp who?
Depp inside dear!

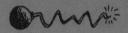

Knock Knock.
Who's there?
Diaz.
Diaz who?
Diaz of our lives.

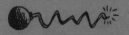

Knock Knock.
Who's there?
Dickon.
Dickon who?
Dickon the right answer.

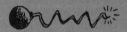

Knock Knock.
Who's there?
Diesel.
Diesel who?
Diesel make you feel better.

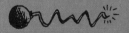

Knock Knock.
Who's there?
Eli.
Eli who?
Elies all the time.

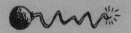

Knock Knock.
Who's there?
Ellen.
Ellen who?
Ellen all the ghouls are after me.

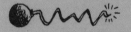

Knock Knock.
Who's there?
Elsie.
Elsie who?
Elsie you in court!

Knock Knock.
Who's there?
Emma.
Emma who?
Emma new neighbor – come round
for tea.

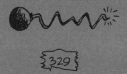

Knock Knock.
Who's there?
Enid.
Enid who?
Enid some shelter from the
ghouls.

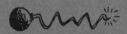

Knock Knock.
Who's there?
Esau.
Esau who?
Esau you in the bath!

Knock Knock.
Who's there?
Evie.
Evie who?
Evie weather.

Knock Knock.
Who's there?
Fang.
Fang who?
Fangs for the memory.

Knock Knock.
Who's there?
Fanta.
Fanta who?
Fanta Claus.

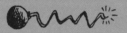

Knock Knock.
Who's there?
Fantasy.
Fantasy who?
Fantasy a walk in the park?

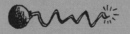

Knock Knock.
Who's there?
Fax.
Fax who?
Fax you very much.

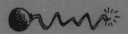

Knock Knock.
Who's there?
Felipe.
Felipe who?
Felipe bath – I need a wash!

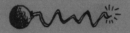

Knock Knock.
Who's there?
Felix.
Felix who?
Felix his bottom again I'll scream!

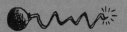

Knock Knock.
Who's there?
Fergie.
Fergie who?
Fergiedness sake let me in!

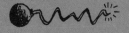

Knock Knock.
Who's there?
Fruit.
Fruit who?
Fruit of all evil.

Knock Knock.
Who's there?
Furry.
Furry who?
Furry's a jolly good fellow!

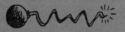

Knock Knock.
Who's there?
Galway.
Galway who?
Galway you silly boy.

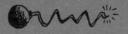

Knock Knock.
Who's there?
Gandhi.
Gandhi who?
Gandhi come out to play?

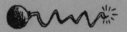

Knock Knock.
Who's there?
Gaskill.
Gaskill who?
Gaskills if it's not turned off.

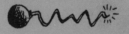

Knock Knock.
Who's there?
Gazza.
Gazza who?
Gazza kiss.

Knock Knock.
Who's there?
Gerald.
Gerald who?
Gerald man from round the corner.

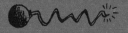

Knock Knock.
Who's there?
Horn.
Horn who?
Horn the way home.

Knock Knock.
Who's there?
Hosanna.
Hosanna who?
Hosanna Claus gets down our tiny
chimney I'll never know!

Knock Knock.
Who's there?
House.
House who?
Hugh's fine thanks. How's John?

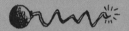

Knock Knock.
Who's there?
Howl.
Howl who?
Howl I know when it's supper time?

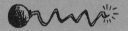

Knock Knock.
Who's there?
Ice cream.
Ice cream who?
Ice cream loudly.

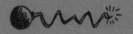

Knock Knock.
Who's there?
Ida.
Ida who?
Ida thought you could say please.

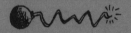

Knock Knock.
Who's there?
Insect.
Insect who?
Insect your name and address
here.

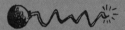

Knock Knock.
Who's there?
Iowa.
Iowa who?
Iowa lot to you.

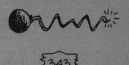

Knock Knock.
Who's there?
Java.
Java who?
Java cat in your house?

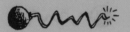

Knock Knock.
Who's there?
Jaws.
Jaws who?
Jaws which one you want.

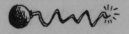

Knock Knock.
Who's there?
Jeanette.
Jeanette who?
Jeanette a big fish this time?

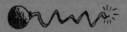

Knock Knock.
Who's there?
Jess.
Jess who?
Jess li'l ol' me.

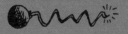

Knock Knock.
Who's there?
Jester.
Jester who?
Jester silly old man.

Knock Knock.
Who's there?
Jewel.
Jewel who?
Jewel know me when you open the door.

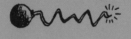

Knock Knock.
Who's there?
Jez.
Jez who?
Jezt a minute.

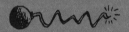

Knock Knock.
Who's there?
Joan.
Joan who?
Joan you know your own daughter?

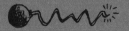

Knock Knock.
Who's there?
June.
June who?
Juneno what time it is?

Knock Knock.
Who's there?
Justine.
Justine who?
Justine the nick of time.

Knock knock.
Who's there?
Karen.
Karen who?
Karen the can for you.

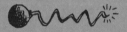

Knock knock.
Who's there?
Keanu.
Keanu who?
Keanu let me in? It's cold out here.

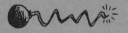

Knock Knock.
Who's there?
Kent.
Kent who?
Kent see without my glasses.

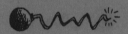

Knock Knock.
Who's there?
Kenya.
Kenya who?
Kenya guess?

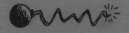

Knock Knock.
Who's there?
Kermit.
Kermit who?
Kermit a crime and you go to jail.

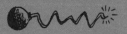

Knock Knock.
Who's there?
Ketchup.
Ketchup who?
Ketchup the tree.

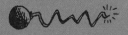

Knock Knock.
Who's there?
Kyoto.
Kyoto who?
Kyoto town tonight!

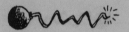

Knock Knock.
Who's there?
Lara.
Lara who?
Lara lara laffs in Liverpool.

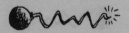

Knock Knock.
Who's there?
Larva.
Larva who?
Larva cup of coffee.

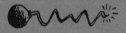

Knock Knock.
Who's there?
Leaf.
Leaf who?
Leaf me be!

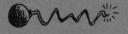

Knock Knock.
Who's there?
Madrid.
Madrid who?
Madrid you wash my sports kit?

Knock Knock.
Who's there?
Maggot.
Maggot who?
Maggot me this new dress today.

Knock Knock.
Who's there?
Maia.
Maia who?
Maianimals are like children to
me.

Knock Knock.
Who's there?
Major.
Major who?
Major answer the door didn't I?

Knock Knock.
Who's there?
Malt.
Malt who?
Maltesers the girls terribly.

Knock Knock.
Who's there?
Mamie.
Mamie who?
Mamie a new dress.

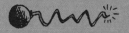

Knock Knock.
Who's there?
Manchu.
Manchu who?
Manchu your food six times.

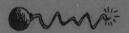

Knock Knock.
Who's there?
Mandy.
Mandy who?
Mandy guns.

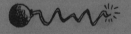

Knock Knock.
Who's there?
Letter.
Letter who?
Letter in!

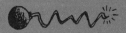

Knock Knock.
Who's there?
Lettuce.
Lettuce who?
Lettuce in and we'll tell you.

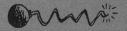

Knock Knock.
Who's there?
Murphy.
Murphy who?
Murphy, have murphy! Don't eat me!

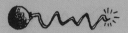

Knock Knock.
Who's there?
Musketeer.
Musketeer who?
Musketeer a doorbell – I'm tired of
knocking.

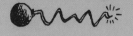

Knock Knock.
Who's there?
Mustard.
Mustard who?
Mustard left it in the car.

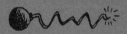

Knock Knock.
Who's there?
Myth.
Myth who?
Myth Thmith thilly!

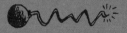

Knock Knock.
Who's there?
Nanny.
Nanny who?
Nanny people are waiting to come in.

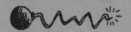

Knock Knock.
Who's there?
Nanny.
Nanny who?
Nanny-one home?

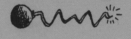

Knock Knock.
Who's there?
Neil.
Neil who?
Neil down before the vampire king!

Knock Knock.
Who's there?
Nell.
Nell who?
Nell is hot.

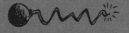

Knock Knock.
Who's there?
Nougat.
Nougat who?
Nougat can go that fast!

Knock Knock.
Who's there?
Oboe.
Oboe who?
Oboe! I've got the wrong house!

Knock Knock.
Who's there?
Oil.
Oil who?
Oil be seeing you.

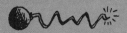

Knock Knock.
Who's there?
Olive.
Olive who?
Olive to regret.

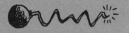

Knock Knock.
Who's there?
Oliver.
Oliver who?
Oliver lone and I'm frightened of
monsters.

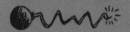

Knock Knock.
Who's there?
Olivier.
Olivier who?
Olivier all my money in my will.

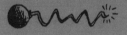

Knock knock.
Who's there?
Opi.
Opi who?
Opi cushion.

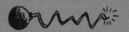

Knock knock.
Who's there?
Orange.
Orange who?
Orange your day to suit the
weather.

Knock Knock.
Who's there?
Panther.
Panther who?
Panther what you wear on your legth.

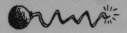

Knock Knock.
Who's there?
Paris.
Paris who?
Paris by the vampire very quietly.

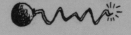

Knock Knock.
Who's there?
Parsley.
Parsley who?
Parsley jam please.

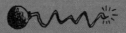

Knock Knock.
Who's there?
Panon.
Panon who?
Panon my intrusion.

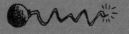

Knock Knock.
Who's there?
Pasta.
Pasta who?
Pasta salt please.

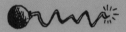

Knock Knock.
Who's there?
Paul and Portia.
Paul and Portia who?
Paul and Portia door to open it.

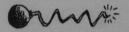

Knock Knock.
Who's there?
Paul.
Paul who?
Paul your weight!

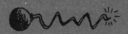

Knock Knock.
Who's there?
Pear.
Pear who?
Pear of shoes.

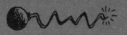

Knock Knock.
Who's there?
Quebec.
Quebec who?
Quebec there if you want a ticket.

Knock Knock.
Who's there?
Queen.
Queen who?
Queen of the crop.

Knock Knock.
Who's there?
Rattlesnake.
Rattlesnake who?
Rattlesnake a big difference!

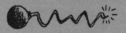

Knock Knock.
Who's there?
Ray.
Ray who?
Rayning cats and dogs.

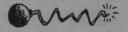

Knock Knock.
Who's there?
Razor.
Razor who?
Razor laugh at that joke.

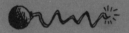

Knock Knock.
Who's there?
Red.
Red who?
Red any good books lately?

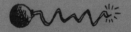

Knock Knock.
Who's there?
Ringo.
Ringo who?
Ringof truth.

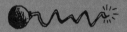

Knock Knock.
Who's there?
Rio.
Rio who?
Riorrange your appointment
please.

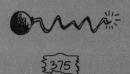

Knock Knock.
Who's there?
Summer.
Summer who?
Summer good, some are bad.

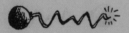

Knock Knock.
Who's there?
Sweden.
Sweden who?
Sweden the pill.

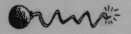

Knock Knock.
Who's there?
Tango.
Tango who?
Tango faster than this you know.

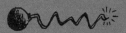

Knock Knock.
Who's there?
Tarzan.
Tarzan who?
Tarzan stripes forever!

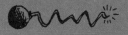

Knock Knock.
Who's there?
Teheran.
Teheran who?
Teheran and look me in the eye.

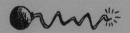

Knock Knock.
Who's there?
Teheran.
Teheran who?
Teheran very slowly – there's a
monster behind you.

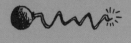